by Joy Nolan
illustrated by Lorinda Bryan Cauley

HOUGHTON MIFFLIN   BOSTON

Copyright © by Houghton Mifflin Company. All rights reserved.

No part of this work may be reproduced or transmitted in any form or by any means, electronic or mechanical, including photocopying or recording, or by any information storage or retrieval system without the prior written permission of Houghton Mifflin Company unless such copying is expressly permitted by federal copyright law. Address inquiries to School Permissions, Houghton Mifflin Company, 222 Berkeley Street, Boston, MA 02116.

Printed in China

ISBN 10: 0-618-88637-0
ISBN 13: 978-0-618-88637-1

56789 0940 16 15 14 13
4500411350

Ed gathered nuts.
He found them for his friends.

How many friends does Ed have?

Ana gathered nuts.
She found them for her friends.

How many friends does Ana have?

Ana gives each friend a nut.
Oh! She doesn't have enough.

How many nuts does Ana have?

Ed gives each friend a nut.
He has too many.

How many nuts does Ed have in all?   **5**

Ed gives a nut to Ana's friend.
Now all the friends have nuts.

6   Who else needs a nut?

Ed gives Ana one too.
Now everyone has a nut!

Squirrel Picnic

Draw Monitor Clarify
1. Look at page 6.
2. Draw 1 nut for everyone in the story.

Tell About
1. Look at pages 2 and 3.
2. Tell someone what Ed and Ana gathered.

Write
1. Look at page 7.
2. Write how many nuts Ed gave Ana.